Reservoirs In The Valley Of The Nile

Society Preservation Monuments Egypt

Reservoirs In The Valley Of The Nile

2018 Reprint Edition by:

Blacklegacypress.org

ISBN: 978-1-63652-467-2

RESERVOIRS

IN THE

VALLEY OF THE NILE

PREPARED FOR THE COMMITTEE OF THE SOCIETY
FOR THE PRESERVATION OF THE MONUMENTS
OF ANCIENT EGYPT.

" There is perhaps no one thing which the most Polite part of mankind have
more universally agreed in, than the vallue they have ever set upon the
Remains of distant Times. Nor among the severall kinds of those Antiquitys
are there any so much regarded as those of Buildings: some for their
magnificence or curious workmanship and others, as they move more lively
and pleasing Reflections (than History without their aid can do) on the Persons
who have inhabited them: on the remarkable things which have been tran-
sacted in them, or the extraordinary occasions of erecting them."—*Sir John
Vanburgh.*

London:

KENNY & CO., PRINTERS, 25 CAMDEN ROAD, N.W.

1894.

RESERVOIRS

IN THE

VALLEY OF THE NILE.

The passage printed on the title page (copied from an article by the Duke of Marlborough in the Summer number of the Pall Mall Magazine of this year) was written by Sir John Vanburgh. He was pleading for the preservation of Woodstock Manor House, which was to be destroyed on his being commissioned to build Blenheim Palace. But his words might almost be described as prophetical, so applicable are they to the present day, when a project is on foot for the formation of a great reservoir at Assuân, which will have the effect of submerging the Island of Philæ, of destroying its splendid buildings with all their historic association, and of destroying also many other great and interesting remains of ancient Egyptian civilization and art in the Valley of the Nile.

The importance of the object which it is desired to attain, that of improving and extending existing means of irrigation in Egypt, will not be disputed. Measures to that effect have indeed been under consideration for a considerable time past. Under the auspices of Mohammad Ali, the founder of the existing dynasty, an important step was taken, some fifty years ago, by the construction of a dam at the apex of the Delta, on the plans and under the superintendence of a distinguished French engineer, Mougel Bey. The Barrage, by which name it is best known, did not at first fulfil the expectations of its designer, owing, it is only just to add, to causes for which he cannot be held responsible. Since the English occupation it has been turned to good account, but its usefulness is necessarily confined to the Delta. Middle and Upper Egypt, or rather, it should be said, the country and valley that extend from below Cairo to the first cataract, a distance by river of nearly 600 miles, derive no benefit whatever from Mougel Bey's important work. Since then further advance in the same direction has become more and more pressing, and the problem which it is now proposed to solve is that of providing perennial irrigation to the whole of Egypt, of creating that is to say, by artificial means, conditions under which the country shall enjoy throughout the whole year, the advantages it at present receives only during the comparatively short season of the Nile flood. The method it has been decided to employ for the attainment of that object, is the construction of a reservoir for the storage of an immense volume of water, destined to supply the deficiencies of the period of low Nile.

Mr. W. Willcocks, M.Inst.C.E., assisted by a staff of engineers, native and foreign, was entrusted by the Egyptian Government with the task of studying the question and of advising the Government in the selection of one or other of the sites that have been recommended. It became accordingly his duty to consider a proposal for the construction of a dam at a point of the Nile restricted to the country between Wadi Halfa and Cairo, and of forming the reservoir in the valley of the river itself. Also to investigate and pronounce an opinion upon a further suggestion, that of utilizing a depression in the desert, known as the Wadi Rayyân, and of converting it into the required reservoir.

The results of the inquiry have been embodied in a most able Report by Mr. Willcocks, and in a masterly summary of the case, from the pen of Mr. W. E. Garstin, Under Secretary of State for the Public Works Department of the Egyptian Government.

In the Wadi Rayyân project, first proposed by Mr. Cope Whitehouse, the required reservoir would be provided by a depression in the neighbourhood of the Fayyûm, 670 square kilometres in extent. It would be filled by means of a canal when the Nile is in flood, and the waters accumulated in the upper levels of the lake would be passed back into the river in the season of the latter's lowest supply. Wadi Rayyân would in short be a counterpart of Lake Mœris, constructed by the rulers of Ancient Egypt some forty to fifty centuries ago. The accompanying map will be sufficient to enable the reader to follow here and elsewhere the brief explanations offered in these pages. It is admitted that Mr. Cope Whitehouse's "brilliant and original suggestion," to use the words applied to it by Sir Benjamin Baker, offers certain great advantages. It is free from all element of danger through the sudden bursting of a dam. No part of the Egyptian or of the Nubian valley would be destroyed by being made to serve as a reservoir, nor would the great losses to archæology, involved in the adoption of the other proposed sites, be inflicted upon Egypt and upon the scientific world. But the conclusion arrived at by the Government Engineers, and by the technical commission of which Sir Benjamin Baker was the English member, was recorded against the project, and attention concentrated upon the question of a dam across the Nile.

Owing to the present political condition of the country beyond Wadi Halfa, the inquiry has been confined to the country below the second cataract. Dal (about half-way between the second and third cataracts) offers, it is admitted, certain advantages, but, Mr. Garstin remarks, it is beyond the existing Egyptian frontier, and at present inaccessible for study.

The sites reported upon by Mr. Willcocks and by the majority of the technical commission, are Silsileh, somewhat over forty miles below Assuân, Assuân itself, and Kalabsha, the latter described as about thirty (forty ?) miles above the first cataract.

Silsileh, it is admitted, offers several favourable features, but the rock is sandstone, said to be of varying consistency, and such as would not afford the uniformly secure foundation to be found in the granite further up the river. With a head of water such as is represented as required for the irrigation of middle and lower Egypt, the reservoir would place the town of Assuân under a depth of water varying from three to seven metres. It need hardly be added that the intervening country would be submerged with all the ancient remains it may contain, including the remarkable temples and ruins of Kom Ombos.

The Assuân Cataract site is that which Mr. Willcocks pronounces to be beyond all comparison the best adapted for his purpose, under the conditions required by the Egyptian Government. He is strongly supported in that opinion by the majority of the technical commission, and Mr. Garstin remarks that he can well understand Mr. Willcocks's enthusiastic advocacy of the site. The rock is hard and compact granite capable of resisting the greatest pressure. The Nile is here broad and shallow, and during the low water season, is divided by numerous islands into many channels, so that measures can easily be adopted whereby the foundations of the dam could be laid in the dry. But with a head of water such as is stated to be required for the irrigation of middle and lower Egypt, the Island of Philæ, of which so much has been heard in connection with the question of Nile reservoirs, would, with all its ancient buildings, be submerged for several months of the year. The Island and its surroundings in their natural features alone, form a scene of remarkable beauty, in no small degree enhanced by the noble and picturesque building with which the island is crowned. Not only can nothing in Egypt be compared with it, but it may be doubted whether throughout the world a spot could be found where beauty, imparted by art as well as by nature, is so singularly combined with objects of deep historic and scientific interest. In addition to the great temple of Isis, a splendid memorial of the Ptolemæic period, that is to say of Greek rule in Egypt, the island contains, or rather it should be said is covered with remains, of which some are of much earlier date. In like manner traces are to be found of the early Christians, who appear to have made use of a portion of the temple for their religious services, and close by are to be found inscriptions showing that the rites of the ancient Egyptian religion were still practised at Philæ in the middle of the fifth century, hardly more than a century and a half before the Mohammedan conquest.

To devastate the Island of Philæ is nothing less than to rudely tear an important leaf out of the sadly mutilated volume upon which almost alone, scholars and students can rely in their laborious endeavours to trace the origin and early history of our modern civilization. On the proposals to demolish the temple and to rebuild it elsewhere, or to hoist it up beyond reach of an artificial inundation, it is hardly necessary to speak. Their originators have perhaps ere this perceived that such ideas are based upon a complete misunderstanding.

On this point, nevertheless, it would be interesting to know precisely what Sir Benjamin Baker proposes when he speaks of raising "the Temples" of Philæ. Supposing such a scheme necessary as the only alternative to submersion, nothing short of raising the whole Island, the area of which as has been shown, is about equal to that of St. James's Park, would meet the case. Does Sir Benjamin Baker mean this? and does he calculate that it can be done for £200,000?

The threatened destruction of Philæ would not be the only result of the proposed dam at Assuân, and the dismay with which it was heard of, was exchanged for absolute consternation, when it came to be understood that the reservoir would extend to a distance of at least one hundred miles up the valley; in other words that the whole of Lower Nubia, its villages, its cultivated and uncultivated lands, and its archæological remains were to be drowned.

An alternative proposal to build the dam at the southern end of the Island of Philæ has been considered, but has been abandoned on account of the inferior nature of the rock on the right bank of the river. It would leave Philæ and its temples untouched, though not under wholly favourable conditions, and in other respects it would produce the same disastrous results as the Assuân project.

The fourth proposed site is that at Kalabsha. The weak point here is the great depth of the right hand channel, where the foundations would have to be laid under a head of nineteen metres of water. It has been argued in favour of the Kalabsha site that it involves less serious losses to archæology. It may be so, but the work of destruction would nevertheless be very great. Not only would the splendid temple of Kalabsha be lost, but the country extending up to Toski, below Ibsambul, a distance of nearly 120 miles, would be laid under water and its ancient remains at Dendûr, Kostamneh, Dakkah, Kubbân, Kurteh, al-Muharraka, Dayr and Aniba would be submerged and soon destroyed.

Here again, therefore, the destruction of a large portion of Nubia comes into question. It is not therefore the antiquities of the country alone that would be submerged and consequently destroyed.

The engineer's maps show that a careful survey with levels has been taken of Silsileh, Philæ, and Kalabsha, the possible places where dams might be constructed. The rest of the map, showing the valley which would be submerged, gives but few indications of a careful survey. The levels taken are at considerable intervals, and there is nothing to indicate by contour lines or otherwise how much of the valley with its numerous villages would be submerged.

The responsibility of carrying out this work, if it be done, will really rest with England; but as yet we have received no assurance that, from a strategic point of view, it is safe to place the security of the whole of Egypt, from Assuân northward, in a position that is certainly not without peril. It is not the engineer's business to consider this question, as is very honestly said in the report, but it is incumbent upon England to do so. In no other country but Egypt would it be possible to destroy so much by one act.

Mr. Garstin points out that, according to the intention of the engineers, when the reservoir is fullest the Nile bed is most empty, and that the partial failure of the dam might make a flood which would rise to some three metres (more than 9 feet) at Cairo, a distance of 580 miles from its source.

At present the cultivable area of Nubia is small. The neglect of centuries has permitted large tracts of land to go to waste. In the neighbourhood of Dakkeh and Korteh are level tracts of considerable extent, and evidently at one time under cultivation. The evidences given us by the numerous remains of towns and temples from Assuân to Anibeh is sufficient to prove that at one time there were flourishing communities all along the river side. Is it politic for Egypt to condemn this district to devastation?

We ask that a subject so important to the present and future welfare of a country under the protection of England, may be considered more fully and exhaustively than it yet seems to have been.

The engineers have set forth the case from their point of

view. The technical commission consisting of three more engineers, were, as Mr. Garstin states, to report on the Reservoirs project, upon the stability of the proposed structures, and the most suitable places. The wider questions were not submitted to them, but these questions are of the most vital importance to Egypt and the responsibility of England cannot be overrated.

Every one must rejoice at the prospect of modern science being used as an effectual means for largely adding to the agricultural wealth of Egypt. But the responsibilities of this country cannot be so limited as to allow our eyes to be closed, or insufficient attention to be directed to all but one aspect of the case. We fully admit its importance, and it is not our purpose to complain of engineers or others interested in the realization of a great undertaking. We are on the contrary disposed to sympathize with men, to whose imagination a great feat of engineering science and skill must naturally appeal with almost irresistible force. But we cannot willingly abandon the hope that even they may find methods whereby to combine important material gains with other great ends.

The cost of the Assuân and of the Kalabsha dams, exclusive of canals and other supplementary works, was estimated by the Government engineers at about the same amount in either case, namely, about £1,600,000 to £1,700,000. The estimate for Assuân has been increased by the technical commission to nearly £2,000,000, in order chiefly to provide for increased security by means of certain modifications. The plans originally proposed for the Kalabsha dam would doubtless require alterations of a similar character, but the additional cost is not stated, and it is not certain that it can be sought in certain figures, somewhat vaguely given by Sir Benjamin Baker, in an article he contributed to the May number of the *Nineteenth Century*. He says in one place that the Kalabsha dam would cost " several millions of pounds " more than that at Assuân ; and in a second passage, that if some other site than Assuân be adopted, the British Parliament should be induced to contribute the extra cost of "three to four millions." But it may be supposed that these passages were meant by the writer to be understood as of a rhetorical character rather than as sober statements of fact.

The proposed Nile reservoir will, we are assured, increase the value of land in Middle Egypt by £23,150,000, and in Upper Egypt by £23,000,000; in the province of Gizeh by £700,000. The increase of value in the Delta is not mentioned, but the annual benefit is reckoned at £3,290,000. The annual increase of produce in Middle and Lower Egypt alone—the reservoir projects which concern the irrigation of Upper Egypt being for the present abandoned—will, it is reckoned, amount to upwards of eight millions stérling. These figures, which are given in detail in Mr. Willcocks' report, are, as Mr. Garstin readily admits, startling; but the problem, we are assured, has been worked out with every care by men of great experience in agricultural questions in Egypt, and, as Mr. Garstin justly observes, a very considerable deduction might be made and yet leave an exceedingly large margin of profit to the country. Mr. Garstin, it must be added, warns his readers moreover that he is dealing with an eventual increase, which will not be felt at once, but "will take years to arrive at." But it is nevertheless to be remarked that an increase of produce of £8,000,000 per annum represents, at twenty-five years purchase, the capital sum of £200,000,000. It is surely not unreasonable to ask that some small portion of the enormous gains the country is to acquire be applied to the preservation of its matchless monuments.

It is not in our power to suggest any particular engineering works, or to recommend any one project from the agricultural point of view or on its engineering merits, in preference to another. But the question has been asked whether a favourable site might not be found to the south of the second cataract. Political considerations put this at the present moment out of the question, but there is a general belief that existing conditions on the Upper Nile cannot be of much longer duration and that the time is fast approaching when Egypt will find herself compelled to re-establish her rule over the upper course of the river, as far probably as Khartûm. The concluding words of Mr. Garstin's note may here perhaps be usefully quoted:

"I myself trust that a reservoir will ere long be a feature in the irrigation system of Egypt, and that the successful completion of one work will have such marked effects on the agricultura. prosperity of the country, that the Government will be encouraged to undertake even bolder schemes. At the head of the second Cataract we have a possible site for storing water, and at the third Cataract it may be possible to so regulate the high floods of the river as to protect Egypt from every fear of inundation. I think, then, we may confidently predict that, if a reservoir be successfully constructed, it will be only one of a chain which will eventually extend from the first Cataract to the junction of the White and Blue Niles at Khartûm. This question, however, is beyond the scope of the present note, in which I have most strictly confined myself to a consideration of the country north of Wadi Halfa."

A question raised as to the immediate necessity for so vast a scheme seems hardly to have received the full consideration it deserves. A doubt has been expressed as to the expediency of commencing with the construction of a dam and storage reservoir of such enormous capacity. After the dam is built, much else will remain to be done and many years must elapse, as is admitted by Mr. Garstin (see above page 10), before the country can be in a position to utilize more than a portion of the immense volume of water proposed to be immediately placed at its disposal. It is natural to ask whether it were not better to proceed more gradually. Cost might thus be spread over a greater number of years, during which the good effects of the works would be gradually brought into operation, and certain dangers, which cannot be altogether disregarded, would be avoided or at least greatly diminished.

Sir Benjamin Baker has justly remarked that the word *impossible* is often exceedingly useful in relation to practical problems. But he will admit that it may be too hastily adopted. One cannot help remembering that Egypt itself offers us a standing example in the existence of the Suez Canal, true as it is that it furnishes us also an example of the almost incredible difference there may be in great engineering undertakings, between original estimates and eventual cost.

On one point there is, we have reason to believe, general concurrence. An exhaustive archæological survey ought to be undertaken of any portion of the Nile valley threatened with destruction, and it is gratifying to know that Mr. Garstin has recommended the Egyptian Government to devote a sum of £50,000 to the purpose.

We again repeat that we are far from desiring to raise obstacles to projects calculated to promote the well-being of the Egyptian people. That object has, on the contrary, our earnest good wishes, and we do not hesitate to admit that under the pressure of absolute necessity, other interests must give way to it. But we claim that the necessity for so great a sacrifice be beyond all reasonable doubt, and that the sacrifice must be jealously restricted to what is clearly shown to be inevitable.

There is one more point which, before concluding, may be usefully touched upon. Much support is undoubtedly attracted in England to the present project, through a widely spread belief that it will, above all things, have the result of improving the condition of the peasantry, with whose hard lot visitors to Egypt are so painfully impressed. It is very generally believed that the peasant labours and suffers under a crushing weight imposed upon him by the land assessment, the land tax as it is not quite correctly called. It is true that the land assessment in Egypt stands in great need of reform. Many landowners pay at a rate far below the average that prevails throughout the country, much lower than that for which the quality and other favourable conditions of their land are a fair equivalent. Others again, chiefly among the poorer class, are charged with a rate far above the average. But speaking generally, the man who holds land directly from the Government is well off. If exceptions be met with, it will for the most part be found that they are men who hold so small a plot that even if they held it free from the *Kharâj*, their lot would still be a hard one. The man, on the other hand, whose condition justly excites the compassion of the foreign visitor, belongs to a numerous class who own no land and who pay no land tax. He earns his living either as a labourer, at a very low wage, on land over which he has no rights of property, or he holds a plot as tenant, for which, under the pressure of competition, he pays, under one form or another, a rent far in excess of the " tax " for which the owner is answerable to the Government.

The Inspectors General of irrigation calculate that the projected irrigation works will produce an increase in rental not far short of double what it is at present. The annual increase for Upper and Middle Egypt alone is estimated at £3,790,777. The probable increase in the Delta is not given. The great landowners are eager to see the irrigation project carried into effect. It is less easy to estimate to what extent the bulk of the peasantry will be benefited.

There are those who hold that the lot of the fellah if his services are exploited for the benefit of large planters of cotton and sugar, will be worse than at present. Time alone can show whether this view or that which is held by the promoters of this immense irrigation scheme is the true one; but when endeavour is made to silence all objections made in the interest of art, history, and archæology on the plausible ground of the immense benefit which is to accrue to the poor cultivators of the soil, it would be as well to take into consideration whether these sanguine prophecies are likely to be fulfilled.

But both the existing classes, large owners and peasants, are, it is urged, equally indifferent to the preservation of the archæological remains that have survived the effects of time and of the ignorance and violence of many generations of men. It is not possible to say how long that indifference is destined to prevail, but this we know, that the ancient monuments of Egypt are the priceless heirloom of its people, and one for which this country stands at the present time in the position of trustee.

APPENDIX.

Subjects of Archæological, Historical and Artistic interest, that would be submerged by a Reservoir with the dam on the First Cataract, called in the report of the Engineer the Assuân Dam.

The Island of Philæ.

Upon this stands the Temple of Isis, the centre of the group of buildings which date from the time of Nectanebo (4th c. B.C.), to that of Diocletian (end of 3rd c. A.D.). Among these buildings are the long corridor of columns leading from the small temple of Nectanebo to the Pylon of the Temple of Isis. The Kiosk or Pharaoh's Bedstead of the time of Tiberias. The small triumphal arch of the time of Diocletian. The quay walls with which the Island is surrounded and which are in part older than any of the remaining temples, in part Ptolemaic and in part Roman. The reservoir being full, the water would submerge everything.

The temple walls are not only covered with sculptures still in excellent preservation and retaining much of their original colour, and with hieroglyphic inscriptions, but are also covered with graffiti left by pilgrims to the shrine, and of the most extreme historic value. There are also numerous Coptic remains.

Inscriptions on neighbouring rocks.

These date back to the XI. and XII. dynasties. They are in most cases at a sufficiently low level to be submerged by this reservoir.

Temple at Biggeh.

On this Island are the remains of a temple older than any on the Island of Philæ. It is supposed that Biggeh was a sacred place before Philæ.

Temple at Debôd.

A temple stands here still well preserved, except in parts which have been shaken down by an Earthquake in 1868, a bad omen for the proposed dam. It is surrounded by a girdle wall of masonry, within which are three large doorways leading directly to the façade. The remains of a great approach from the river are still in fair preservation. The

whole stands on river deposit, and would fall to pieces as
soon as submerged. The temple is of the time of the
Ptolemies, and bears on its walls the name of one of the
dynasty of native Kings, who reigned in Nubia during the
period of the Ptolemies and the Roman Emperors.

Here are the remains of a small Ptolemaic temple. The *Gertassa.*
basement wall on which it stands would be submerged, and
would soon yield. Close by are large quarries of fine sandstone. These contain a vast number of inscriptions and
graffiti, chiefly Greek, and dating from Roman imperial
times. From this quarry the stones for Philæ were taken.
South of the quarries are walls of masonry inclosing a large
area. A temple stood within. The gateways are ingeniously
arranged for defence, whilst the walls retain in their thick-
ness, stairs leading to the top for the use of the garrison.
This work is probably Roman.

Here stands a small but very perfect little temple, and *Tefah.*
about it are the remains of several houses of stone, almost *(Taphis of the Itinerarium Antonini.)*
unique. They are of late Ptolemaic or Roman work.

The most magnificent structure in Nubia. It retains its *Temple at Kalabsha.*
quay walls, stairs of approach, and vast surrounding walls of *(Talmis.)*
masonry, in a condition more complete than any other
temple in Egpyt. A pylon wider than the front of West-
minster Abbey stands on the upper terrace, and leads into
the great courtyard. and temple. The site was sacred in the
XVIII. dynasty. The existing structure is Roman, using in
part Ptolemaic remains. The walls are very perfect with
their sculpture, the roofs only having fallen in. In the
courtyard are a vast number of graffiti, many of which have
yet to be cleared and deciphered. They extend down to
about A.D. 540, when Silko, the Christian King of the
Nobades, defeated the Blemmyes, and recorded his exploit on
the temple walls.

Here is a very perfect little Temple of Ptolemaic times, *Dendur.*
with the interior full of wall sculptures and inscriptions,
which are of particular interest. It stands above a very well
preserved terrace. To the North. lie the remains of the
ancient town.

The remains of a great rectangular fort of sun-dried bricks. *Koshtemneh.*
It forms one. of a chain of ancient forts through Nubia,

extending to Semneh, south of the Second Cataract. The external dimensions are 304 feet by 252. The walls 12 feet thick. The remains of a temple, probably of the XIX. dynasty, can be traced within the enclosure, whilst numerous ancient brick buildings, probably of the same date as the fort lie around outside.

Dakkeh (Pselchis). This is one of the best preserved temples in Nubia. The pylon is absolutely perfect. The temple itself is covered with sculpture and inscriptions. The cartouches of Thothmes III. and Seti I., taking us back to the XVIII. dynasty, have been found. The existing temple is chiefly the work of the native king Ergamenes, and also of the Ptolemies and Roman Emperors.

Kübban (contra Pselchis). Opposite Dakkeh stands the great brick fort of Kubban. This great structure is of ancient brickwork, with the walls 18 feet thick, and in parts 25 feet high. Names of kings of the XII. dynasty have been found immediately to the south, and the ruins of the temple within the area of the walls seem to be of the XVIII. or XIX. dynasty. The fort commanded the road to the gold mines. With the exception of the walls round the city of El Kab, Kubban is the most complete fortress north of the Second Cataract.

Korteh. Here are remains of an ancient city with masses of pottery.

Muharragah (Hierascaminos) Here are ruins of a temple of late date. On the walls are many graffiti in Greek and hieroglyphic sculptures and inscriptions yet to be made out.

Other ruins of less interest are shown on the accompanying map.

The waters of the reservoir would extend to Korosko, if the dam be constructed at Philæ. They will extend further South, at least to Anibeh, if the dam be constructed at Kalabsha. In this event, the fort and ancient town opposite **Eleseyih.** Eleseyih will be submerged, and probably the rock excavation at Eleseyih itself; but the chief loss would be the **Anibeh.** great mass of ancient tombs at Anibeh.

Here are still standing brick pyramidal tombs probably of the XII. dynasty, some retaining within them their ancient wall painting. Graves under cairns or surrounded by rings of stone are numerous.

The foregoing list of antiquities is by no means exhaustive.

www.ingramcontent.com/pod-product-compliance
Lightning Source LLC
Chambersburg PA
CBHW031450070426
42452CB00037B/591